Animal Families

Bobbie Kalman

🌳 Crabtree Publishing Company

www.crabtreebooks.com

Created by Bobbie Kalman

For Marion
You have become a very important part of my life.
I am so grateful to have found you.

Author and Editor-in-Chief
Bobbie Kalman

Editors
Reagan Miller
Robin Johnson

Photo research
Crystal Sikkens

Design
Bobbie Kalman
Katherine Kantor
Samantha Crabtree (cover)

Production coordinator
Katherine Kantor

Illustrations
Barbara Bedell: pages 11, 24 (raccoons and sea horse)
Katherine Kantor: page 6
Bonna Rouse: page 24 (eggs, turtle hatching, and sea turtle)
Margaret Amy Salter: pages 7, 24 (penguin and wolf)
Tiffany Wybouw: page 5

Photographs
© BigStockPhoto.com: pages 6, 12, 13 (bottom)
© iStockphoto.com: pages 1, 18, 21 (top), 23 (top left and right)
© 2008 Jupiterimages Corporation: page 16
© ShutterStock.com: back cover, pages 3, 4, 5, 8, 9, 10, 13 (top), 14,
    15, 17, 24 (horse, fox nursing, and quokka)
Other images by Corel, Creatas, Iconotec, and Digital Vision

Library and Archives Canada Cataloguing in Publication

Kalman, Bobbie, 1947-
    Animal families / Bobbie Kalman.

(Introducing living things)
Includes index.
ISBN 978-0-7787-3226-6 (bound).--ISBN 978-0-7787-3250-1 (pbk.)

    1. Familial behavior in animals--Juvenile literature. I. Title.
II. Series.

QL761.5.K34 2007   j591.56'3   C2007-904234-1

Library of Congress Cataloging-in-Publication Data

Kalman, Bobbie.
    Animal families / Bobbie Kalman.
      p. cm. -- (Introducing living things)
    Includes index.
    ISBN-13: 978-0-7787-3226-6 (rlb)
    ISBN-10: 0-7787-3226-6 (rlb)
    ISBN-13: 978-0-7787-3250-1 (pb)
    ISBN-10: 0-7787-3250-9 (pb)
    1. Familial behavior in animals--Juvenile literature. I. Title. II. Series.

QL761.5.K35 2007
591.56'3--dc22
                                        2007026962

Crabtree Publishing Company

www.crabtreebooks.com   1-800-387-7650

Published in Canada
Crabtree Publishing
616 Welland Ave.
St. Catharines, Ontario
L2M 5V6

Published in the United States
Crabtree Publishing
PMB16A
350 Fifth Ave., Suite 3308
New York, NY 10118

Published in the United Kingdom
Crabtree Publishing
White Cross Mills
High Town, Lancaster
LA1 4XS

Published in Australia
Crabtree Publishing
386 Mt. Alexander Rd.
Ascot Vale (Melbourne)
VIC 3032

Contents

Different families

People belong to different kinds of families. Some families have two parents, and some have one. Some families have two mothers and two fathers. Some families have one child, whereas other families have many children.

Animal families are different, too. In some animal families, both parents care for their babies. Parents feed their babies and protect them from danger. These duck parents are caring for their baby ducks.

This mother sea turtle is laying eggs in the sand. She will then leave the eggs. Baby turtles will **hatch** from the eggs. The babies will have to feed and protect themselves.

Father helpers

Most animal mothers do all the work of carrying their eggs and laying them, but a few fathers do help! A mother sea horse passes her eggs to the father sea horse. The young sea horses live inside their father's **pouch**, or pocket, where they grow.

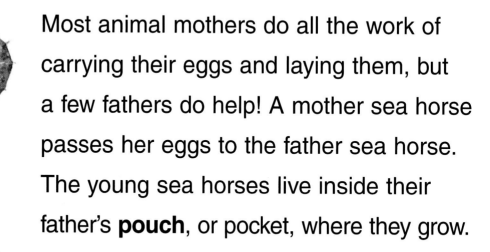

Penguin mothers lay eggs. Some penguin fathers then look after the eggs. They use their bodies to keep the eggs warm. When the babies hatch from the eggs, both parents feed and protect their **chicks**.

egg

chick

Mammal mothers

Mammals are animals with hair or fur on their bodies. Mammal mothers make milk inside their bodies. Their babies drink the milk. Drinking mother's milk is called **nursing**. This baby horse, called a **foal**, is nursing.

Many mammal mothers care for their babies for a long time. They stay close to their babies and keep them safe. Mothers teach their babies how to find food. This mother bear is teaching her baby how to catch fish.

Pouch potatoes

A quokka is a mammal.
A mother quokka has
a pouch on her body.
There is a baby
inside the
pouch.

These animals are koalas. Both quokka babies and koala babies are called **joeys**. A joey lives and nurses in its mother's pouch. When a joey gets bigger, it leaves the pouch, but it lives with its mother for about a year. The mother keeps the joey safe and teaches it to find food.

Adult food

At first, mammal babies drink their mothers' milk. As the babies grow, they start eating adult foods. Babies cannot eat large pieces of food. Some animal parents chew the food and pass it into the mouths of their babies. This jackal mother is passing food into the mouth of its **pup**, or baby.

*This moose mother is showing her **calf** which plants to eat.*

*This baby fox, called a **kit**, has caught its first mouse.*
Its mother helped him catch it. Soon the kit will catch a rabbit.

Keeping clean

A mammal mother **grooms**, or cleans, her baby. This monkey is taking bugs off her baby's fur. Grooming keeps animals healthy. It is also a way that animals show they care for one another.

This mother panda is grooming her cub. Why do you think the cub is laughing?

Hiding their young

Predators are animals that hunt and eat other animals. Predators often hunt young animals. Young animals are easier to catch than older, stronger animals are. Many mothers hide their babies so predators will not find them. A bobcat mother has hidden her kittens in a dead tree log. She will move them if she feels they are in danger.

A deer mother has hidden her **fawn**, or
baby, in the woods. It is hard to see the fawn
because its fur is the same color as the
brown leaves on the forest floor. Hiding the
fawn helps keep it safe from predators.

Wolf packs

A mother wolf gives birth to a **litter** of pups. A wolf litter is a group of four to seven pups. The mother hides the pups in a **den**, or home, for about one month. The pups are safe from predators in the den.

Wolves live in groups called **packs**. The two parent wolves are the leaders of a pack. The father is in charge of hunting. He brings food to the mother and the pups. When the pups are ready to come out of the den, they join the pack. They learn to hunt with their parents. These young wolves are old enough to hunt.

Big groups

Many animals live together in big groups. Elephants travel in groups called **herds**. When elephant babies, called **calves**, are born, they can walk right away. They have to walk to keep up with their herds. The calves stay in the middle of the herds.

Calves are safer with adults around them.
The bigger elephants can protect them from predators.

Dolphins travel together in groups called **schools** *or* **pods**.

These baboons live together in groups called **troups**.

Family ties

How are these animals showing love? How do you show your family that you love them? Does your family enjoy group hugs? Do you give your mother kisses?

Do you laugh and have fun?

*Do you enjoy talking to
your mother or father?*

*Do you dance when
you are happy?*

23

Words to know and Index

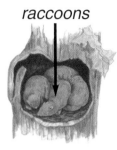
raccoons

den
pages 18, 19

eggs
pages 5, 6, 7

grooming
pages 14-15

hatching
pages 5, 7

mammals
pages 8, 9,
10, 12, 14

nursing
pages 8, 11

penguins
page 7

joey

quokkas
pages 10, 11

pouch

sea horses
page 6

sea turtles
page 5

wolves
pages 18-19

Other index words

bobcats page 16

fawns page 17

foals page 8

food pages 9, 11, 12-13, 19

pouches pages 6, 10, 11

predators pages 16, 17, 18, 20

24

Printed in the U.S.A.